How to Get Over a Crush on a Friend

Cara Menae Miller

Cover design by Cara Menae Miller using stock photo ID 1145438846

The stories in this book are either true or inspired by real stories of myself and people I know. To protect anonymity, identifying details and some circumstantial details were changed. Although the particular stories that inspired this book were friendships between males and females, I believe the insights and lessons in this book absolutely apply to any gender and to any set of genders.

CONTENTS

ACKNOWLEDGMENTS

I thank Sam and Jenifer, who gave me incredibly valuable feedback on the original drafts of this book, helping me improve it greatly.

I thank my mom for guiding me to take out cuss words I really wanted to use (dang it) and for her very helpful edits.

1 THE WORLD TELLS YOU TO MARRY YOUR FRIEND

On the back porch on a grey October 31st, my mom needed to draw lines on my four-year-old face to complete my cat costume. I had a headband with fuzzy black ears, a short black dress with a tail, and braided hair. My mom told me to go inside the house, through our small kitchen and into the bathroom off the hallway.

Inside the top drawer on the right was the eyeliner, she said. "Your dad is taking a shower, but you can knock then go on in."

The door to the bathroom was a symbol of the barrier between me and my dad. I knocked and he said, "Come in," but not in a patient tone, because a patient tone isn't one my dad used.

As I entered, I told him I was getting mom's eyeliner so she could draw whiskers on my face. He said, "Okay."

My young soul understood that my dad didn't want me in the bathroom any more than he had wanted me to come into the world. Yet he wasn't going to say that. His deeper thoughts were obscured, as was his figure behind the shower door as hot water poured over his pale body and coarse red hair.

Amidst the real and symbolic distance between us, I was enveloped in powerful warmth and steam that carried the strong scent of his aftershave. The cologne-scented steam filled a space in my heart as large as the earth, and I was drunk with it. The scent and my dad were one, and I longed for his affection to pour onto me like the shower water poured onto him.

My dad only ever gave me a few crumbs of attention. They were tiny and stale, and I can almost remember each one. They weren't at all like the warm shower water.

Whenever I've stood face to face with a friend I was in love with, I saw a blurred figure behind a shower door; his thoughts, like my dad's, seemed concealed. But his presence in front of me was warm like steam and smelled like my dad's aftershave. I was filled with longing. Though my crush was unrequited, I wanted to soak in the warmth and keep wishing.

I decided in my early 20s to stop dating men "like my dad." So, I pursued friendships with men instead. I look back over my mid 20s and all of my 30s and see a long line of crushes on friends—crushes that did not become relationships. Friendship was a safe way for me to warm myself in the scented steam of men I was attracted to and dream of a day when more than just a scent could be given. Deep down, I knew it probably couldn't be, and that kept me safe. No one could get dumped and no one could get *officially* hurt.

I have gotten good at friendships with single men who may be like my dad in various ways but always were in one important way: they didn't love me back. Yet they did give me attention— much more of it than my dad ever gave.

I knew how to keep it coming. I bubbled with positive energy, gave them fine-tuned attention and compliments, laughed at their jokes and made *them* laugh, engaged them in stimulating conversations, did them favors, and supplied them with drinks and home-cooked food. What guy friend wouldn't come back for more?

Yet my crushes were not harmless. In the murky darkness, underneath my laughter and merriment, I was in a delicate fantasy world that was always at risk of unraveling, exposing the child standing in the bathroom steam in a state of desperate longing.

Because I know it so well, I will share with you in this book the unique fantasy world that accompanies crushing on friends, from five different angles:

- The world tells you to marry your friend.

- You're not sure whether to profess your feelings.

- You never dated and therefore never broke up.

- You don't know whether to keep being friends.

- You're living in a fantasy.

It's time for ominous background music to fade in. Each chapter, beginning with this one, offers *un*inspirational quotes and stories to counteract inspirational ones—you know, the ones on Google Images and Pinterest giving us hope that could turn out to be false.

You picked up this book called, "How to Get Over a Crush on a Friend," so I assume that your crush isn't panning out the way you hoped...

That's not to say that it can't....

but...

Let's begin.

It's hard to get over a crush on a friend when the world tells you to marry your friend.

Danny' Story:

Kerry is 9 years younger than me. We met 11 years ago, when she was 21 and I was 30. We are both painters and met at a gallery in our city. We were looking at the same painting.

Things took a magical turn minutes after we introduced ourselves. I fumbled through an explanation for why I collect paintings of old, abandoned gas stations. In my awkward fumbling, I noticed Kerry was really listening.

"It makes sense," she responded, keeping eye contact with me.

But you don't understand what happened when she said, "It makes sense." I saw that she *got* me deeply, but I can't explain how I knew that.

I then saw a picture in my head of Kerry and me standing inside the front of a church getting married, and I "perceived" that this "would" take place years down the road. She stood facing me in the art gallery as I saw this mental picture, making the experience feel like an intimate moment between us, though she had no idea what I was seeing or feeling.

I decided later that night that what I had experienced was a "vision." Unfortunately, spiritualizing that picture in my head royally screwed me up for many years to come.

This girl is way too pretty and way too cool to become my wife, I thought. I had never seen myself with a girl that men are likely to fight over—a young brunette with arresting eyes and cool clothing and jewelry. I got her phone number before I left the gallery.

I called her a few days later. I was shocked when she agreed to get coffee with me and even more shocked when we became good friends after three hours at Starbucks.

We started getting together at my place and at hers. Kerry was "there" with me in every word I spoke, just as she was at our first meeting in the art gallery. In her presence, time slowed down. Once, as we sat on my couch drinking glasses of Pinot Grigio, I counted each of our inhales for one minute. For every three of my inhales, she had only one. She'd look at me and listen like there was nowhere else she ever wanted to go. I felt entirely seen and heard.

I became her art mentor for her abstract paintings. She took photographs of all kinds of inanimate objects. She'd find one square inch in a photo and paint the tiny section onto a large canvas. I showed her how to paint bolder strokes. I taught her to believe in herself as an artist. She stared into her canvas the same way she stared into me. We started painting together in her studio.

After months of being hopelessly in love with Kerry and believing our romantic future was as sure as each sunrise, I told her what I think she already knew: that I liked her and would prefer to be more than friends. She'll never know what an understatement that was.

She didn't recoil at my words. She was her usual focused self as she looked down for a minute then replied that she didn't know how she felt and would "think about it."

I asked her more questions, hoping to find out whether she liked me in that way or not.

By the end of the conversation, she admitted she didn't.

Kerry's connection to me never flinched even after she knew I liked her. I continued to have a crush on her for several more years.

We are still friends 11 years later, although we have less contact now. When we see each other, it is never different than it was the first time we met: we connect deeply.

You'll hear more from Danny about his crush on Kerry throughout this book. As you can imagine, he has a lot to say about crushes on friends.

Inspirational quotes can be our biggest obstacle to getting over a crush on a friend. Check Google

Images and Pinterest to see where I'm coming from. You'll find quotes telling you to marry your best friend; to build a friendship before marriage; that the best marriages are between best friends. And here's one: "If you have to invite your best friend to your wedding, you are marrying the wrong person." You start feeling like Google and Pinterest have your back—and if *they*'re rooting for you, how can you *not win!*?

Stories of friends marrying each other complement these quotes. We all know these stories, and they keep us hopeful. Here are four of them off the top of my head:

- "I thought he was the biggest dork; he was "un-dateable." But we kept spending time together, playing tennis and going out for coffee. He showed me unconditional love, and my feelings started to change. Three years later, we were engaged."

- "He didn't return my feelings for the first six years we were friends. Then, one day, he did, and he told me."

- "We were friends for a year and a half before he kissed me. But in the time leading up to that kiss, I didn't know if he wanted to be more than friends. I thought the suspense was going to *literally* kill me."

- "He decided he was going to marry me. But the idea of dating him was laughable. Yet after three years of being friends and seeing how good he was with my kids, I fell in love with him."

The four couples in these stories are still married today.

The Friend-Crush Survey

If you have a crush on a friend, feelings of inspiration may be welling up in you right now after reading these quotes.

But I'm not sure which does more damage on the internet: horror stories, or inspirational quotes about friends falling in love.

So, we're taking a 180-degree turn away from hope and toward heartless facts, via the friend-crush survey I created. The survey received 239 respondents: 201 from SurveyMonkey and 38 from Reddit.

The 239 survey respondents had had a total of 967 crushes on friends by the time of the survey. 295 of those friends, or almost 31%, returned the feelings, and 220 of them, or almost 23%, agreed to a romantic relationship. This means that less than a quarter of those crushes on friends led to a shot at love.

The data from this survey lends itself to one of my favorite quotes. Spoiler—this one isn't about marrying your friend.

> *"What screws us up the most in life*
>
> *is the picture in our head of what*
>
> *it's supposed to be."*[i]

I feel the pain of that quote more than I want to. I know Danny does, too, as he *literally* saw a picture in his head of Kerry and him getting married. And he confessed that picture did indeed screw him up in life.

My mind has been screwed up, too. Many times, I have woven together inspirational quotes and others people's love stories into a false reality by imagining that my friend was falling for me. To show you just how far I've come in my recovery,

I have written my very own *un*inspirational quotes—one for each chapter. (You probably won't want these in frames).

 Here's the first one:

Someone else's love story

could be your false reality.

It's not good news. But if you meditate on it, really start to internalize it, you'll be closer to getting over your crush on your friend.

Some people derive satisfaction from imposing their stories onto you. Have you noticed? Their eyes glimmer while they share their story as if it is the objective truth of the universe and bound to happen that way for you.

I'm a highly sensitive person, an HSP. A highly sensitive person picks up on a lot of information and is very attuned to subtleties. So, the subtle message of quotes and stories about friends falling in love is *not lost on me*. Here it is:

By being friends with your crushes, you can make them fall in love with you.

It implies that friendship creates the ideal condition by which unreturned love is eventually "worn down" and gives way to romance. Friendship is some kind of magic elixir—pour enough of it into the pot, for a long enough time, and you end up with an irresistible love potion your friend can't resist.

Maybe you're smart enough not to internalize so much false hope. But I wasn't. I hoped that the more I "aced" friendship with my crushes, the closer they'd get to showing up unexpectedly at my doorstep for our first kiss.

I now get that friendship with a crush isn't a magic elixir.

Do you want some proof? You'll read several stories in this book about crushes on friends based on the true stories of myself and a few people I know. And here are just some things we did for our friends that didn't make them fall in love with us:

- Surprise him with homemade mug cakes in matching ornate ceramic mugs (his jaw dropped).

- Engage in repeated deep, life-altering, soulmate-like conversations.

- Flirt just a tad bit with his single friends in hopes of inciting jealousy.

- Go on hiking trips for entire weekends and respectfully stay *in my own bed* in our shared cabin (torture).

- You've heard this one already: paint together (is there anything *more* romantic?)

- Be cool and collected, as if perfectly indifferent to the outcome of the friendship.

- Make the right amount of eye contact and keep an open posture... you know, since up to 80% of our communication is body language...

- Send adorable birthday cards and happy birthday Bitmojis every freaking year.

- Edit his resume so he can actually get a job, taking care to remove "Dungeons and Dragons" from the *Skills* section.

- Go on vacations with his family and make them all love me. (*How could that not work!?*)

Things like this taught my friends and me that all the friendship in the world won't make someone fall in love with us.

Friendship can provide an awesome opportunity for falling in love. And sometimes friendship is the only opportunity for people to have the time and connection they need to fall in love.

But... I don't believe friendship *makes* someone fall in love.

Why do I believe this?

Years and years of experiences, the ones that led me to write this book. And not just my experiences.

If your crush isn't going to fall in love with you, then your crush isn't going to fall in love with you, even if you two are good friends for a lifetime. Romantic love develops for reasons we don't quite understand, involving factors not quite in our control, and even an amazing friendship that won't *necessarily* crack that nut.

I'm so happy for friends who fall in love with each other. Their stories are beautiful. I wish one of their stories were mine.

Perhaps you wish that for yourself, too. But don't let someone else's love story become your false reality. Don't let them take you out of your reality and into theirs. Because you can't go there, no matter how much you want to.

Don't worry, you'll have your own story. I don't know what it will be. But I do know it will be yours, and that will make it beautiful.

2 YOU'RE NOT SURE WHETHER TO PROFESS YOUR FEELINGS

Being in love with a friend who doesn't love us back means that we are not on the same page, but we can both fantasize that we are.

He can fantasize that I'm perfectly content to just be his friend. I can fantasize that, at the end of the day, I'm the woman he's going to choose.

My millions of musings about my longest crush, Ryan, were pointless for one reason: he and I were never on the same page.

Ryan and I met on a lawn at graduate school. Two years later, we were talking for hours on the same lawn and even in the same spot where we'd met. I doubt he remembers meeting me, though.

I love redheads, which could have something to do with my dad being one. Ryan's soft, straight auburn hair was just red enough. He is a handsome cross between Harry Potter and John Lennon. Ryan is a poet and, learning I was a writer, he asked me if I would help him refine his "spoken word poetry" for a class project.

We met at his dining room table weekly as I helped him brainstorm and reword lines for the poem he'd recite in class at the end of the semester.

I have a thing for guys who can sit still in the moment, and Ryan was as still as a pond on a windless day. He listened to each word I said as if he was pinning a butterfly—he'd lock eyes with me and think long about each of my suggestions as my heart fluttered and my body got still.

Afterwards he would actually *cook* for me, excelling at well-seasoned rice and vegetable stir-fries complemented by hard apple cider from his fridge. We discovered we both loved hiking and made our first plan to hike together that weekend.

Two months into our blooming friendship, I was torn up about whether to tell Ryan just a *little bit* of the truth that I was madly in love with him.

I thought he would have made a move by then, but he hadn't. Even after some of our friends at school said they noticed a special way he looked at me. Even after being the only girl he spent hours of one-on-one time with. Even after we went hiking three times, one of those time being a whole weekend away camping in a cabin—*just the two of us.*

I was tormented by the question mark in my heart. Did he feel the same way? I got to the point of actually fretting. And I know what I need to do when I fret: something.

I decided that "something" would be to understate my feelings to him after we finished working on his poem. My feelings *needed* to be understated, because I had never been so smitten with a guy before and was even secretly looking at engagement rings.

We sat down on a park bench after he practiced reciting to me the final poem that I'd helped him rework.

"I wanted to talk with you about helping you with your project," I said. And I think he thought we were going to talk about his poem.

Then I continued with my very well-rehearsed line:

"Working on your poem together felt like a bonding experience. It made me wonder if you still just want to be friends."

He did not seem uncomfortable. He looked down to think. "I don't know what the future holds for us," he said.

"Is there another girl?" I said.

"No."

"Are you saying there *might* be a future for us someday?"

He looked down again and said, "I think I just see you as a friend... I hope we can keep being friends?"

Ryan and I have a connection, but it has never been the same one. Our friendship thrives not only on what we say to each other but largely on what we *don't* say.

Because I didn't tell Ryan that I was in love with him. Because he didn't tell me that he was not in love with me. Because he didn't want to say any more than he said that day on the park bench. Because I didn't want to say any more than *I* said that day on the park bench. By keeping our words to a minimum, our friendship could go on, each of us living in our imaginary world of what we hoped it was.

Even after Ryan admitted his lack of feelings, he never stopped looking at me like I fulfilled something in him. He asked me to help him write more poetry. We even did more hiking and camping.

So, after some nights of crying myself to sleep, I timidly stitched my fantasy back together. *Have hope*, I'd tell myself. *He hasn't fallen for me yet. But maybe he will.*

Fantasizing that he'd fall for me felt like living, and the thought of giving up hope felt like dying. So, I lived for the day he would love me back.

Meanwhile, I decided to never say another word to Ryan about my feelings.

My silence protected my fantasy from unraveling any further.

Cara's Story (that's me)

Yes, another story of mine. I have so many....

Jimmy insisted he was going to fulfill his dream of becoming a Catholic priest and taking vows of celibacy. He was going to leave for an overseas seminary "in a year and a half" from the time we met.

Yet Jimmy and I had an instant connection. He is stocky with a long beard and a short ponytail. He has a handsome face and, being from the hills of West Virginia, his grammar is just bad enough to be endearing. He is jolly, and we connected through joking around and sharing similar views.

I helped him as he ran his hand-crafted jewelry business. We went canoeing. He even took me out to eat a couple of times, opening up to me about his fears of going to seminary. He was clear that he "didn't want a relationship with anybody," yet he was flirting with me a little and no doubt liked my attention. Mutual friends of ours would say that Jimmy and I were "really good friends." From my perspective, him falling for me would be the perfect plot twist in his plan to become a celibate priest.

It took me months to profess my feelings for him. When I did, I half hoped he would tell me he wasn't interested so that I could get resolution and closure. But all he said in response was, "You have a lot to offer."

I have a lot to offer? That's it?

It was his way of saying "no" without hurting my feelings. I can't say it helped me give up hope.

Weeks before his departure, Jimmy drank too much—probably living it up a little before embarking on his vocational journey. In his drunken state, he told his best friend that he would marry me if he wasn't going to become a priest, and his best friend told me.

Up until the very day he left for seminary, the suspense was killing me as I hoped Jimmy would change his mind and not get on the plane. I cried and prayed. When Jimmy left, I spent three straight days in so much emotional pain that my stomach hurt. We'd had a friendship, and it was gone... along with my hope of Jimmy staying in town and sweeping me off my feet.

Remember this testimony from Chapter 1?

"We were friends for a year and a half before he kissed me. But in the time leading up to that kiss, I didn't know if he wanted to be more than friends. I thought the suspense was going to *literally* kill me."

Her name is Sarah, and she's married to the man in the story—a guy named Patrick who everyone agrees is a "stud." Sarah loves her love story. I would to, if it were mine. Have you seen Mary Poppins—the scene where Mary Poppins, Bert, and the two kids jump into the chalk drawing and find themselves in an imaginary world of dreams? I wanted to jump into Sarah's love story like they jumped into that drawing.

I was friends with Sarah when she broke off an engagement; when she moved into a new apartment... the one right next to Patrick's; when she and Patrick became good friends; when he first kissed her on their trip to visit his parents; when they got engaged; and when they got married. I helped them when they packed up their apartment to move out east.

Sarah and Patrick believe their story is magical because they played their cards so well. For the year and a half before they kissed, they were "falling in love and not talking about it." Although Sarah felt it might *literally* kill her to stay silent as she worried about the future, she and Patrick now think she did the right thing.

After they were married, I went to Sarah for advice about Jimmy. Sarah told me her love story (again) and emphasized, "We were falling in love and *not talking about it.*" She suggested I do the same: stay silent and let Jimmy fall in love with me.

Sarah hoped the story of me and Jimmy would be like the story of her and Patrick. Remember what I said in the last chapter about people telling their stories as if it's the objective truth of the universe?

Sarah was nice to take the time to listen to my dilemma and to offer me the advice I asked for.

Yet there could be a lot wrong with her advice being applied generally to crushes on friends.

First, recall the reality-check survey from Chapter one. "Falling in love and not talking about it" often amounted to falling into *delusion* and not talking about it, since crushes on friends were not returned in most cases in the survey. In my case, staying silent wasn't helping Jimmy feel anything at all. Although he'd said in a drunken stupor that he'd marry me if he wasn't becoming a priest, not all drunken statements can be trusted. And he did choose, in the end, to become a priest.

Secondly, there is nothing wrong with telling someone you like them. Many relationships begin with romance, not friendship, and work out.

Thirdly, sharing your feelings might help spark a mutual attraction.

Lastly, telling someone how you feel is showing the real you, something you ultimately need to do in any romantic relationship. If telling your friend that you like them will forever ruin their ability to fall in love with you, what does that tell you about your potential with this person?

Telling someone you like them may feel like an impending catastrophe. But the worst it can possibly do is illuminate the truth of what is already going on under the surface.

This leads right into my next *un*inspirational quote:

> *Telling the truth can't make things bad but*
>
> *it can show you how bad*
>
> *things already are.*

I don't believe you need to keep your feelings to yourself in hopes that your mysterious silence will lure your friend to fall in love with you. I'm glad that worked for someone else, but I'm guessing that someone isn't you, since you've picked up this book. Don't live in fear of ruining your friendship or any romance that could develop. Telling the truth can't *make* things bad.

Professing feelings is not a catastrophe. Moreover, doing so may not even bring clarity. Some of my crushes did not give me a direct answer about how they felt in return. Their "no" was hidden behind "I don't know" or "I don't know yet" or "I'm sorry I don't have an answer" or "All I know is that I enjoy spending time with you." Even when they were clear about their unrequited love, that clarity got muddled for me when I kept hearing from them after my profession of feelings: *"Wanna come over tomorrow night?"*

Not knowing whether to profess your feelings can ultimately lead to not knowing, *all over again,* whether to profess your feelings *again.*

I'll let Danny explain this one...

> After Kerry told me she didn't have feelings for me, I had a really hard time accepting it. Just as two watercolor strokes brushed side by side on a canvas bleed into each other slowly, Kerry's unreturned feelings took time to bleed into my sense of reality. I wasn't good at "getting" it, because our one-on-one time continued with the same intimate conversations about art and life while we painted in her studio.
>
> After two more years of friendship, I agonized all over again whether to bring up my feelings for a second time. Our friendship had survived when I told her the first time. But would it survive if I told her again? I didn't

want to come across as not taking no for an answer. And I didn't want to give her a reason to back away from our friendship; I couldn't stand the thought of losing her.

I never did say anything to her again about my feelings, and my confusion remained.

In addition to Jimmy and Ryan, I have told five other friends about my feelings. Two of them returned the feelings and we dated for a time. One of them gave me some sort of amalgam of "I don't know" and "No." One of them gave me a direct "No." Another of them said he didn't know yet, and he asked me out for coffee after thinking about it for a few months. But before our coffee date arrived, he met someone.

I have no regrets about sharing my feelings with these friends and do not feel I lost anything at all by doing so. I believe that each of them appreciated the ego boost if nothing else. One of them distanced himself from me for a few months after I shared my feelings, but that was no real loss of friendship or of anything else.

It's hard to get over a crush on a friend when you're not sure whether to profess your feelings.

You can profess them if you want to. It can show you how bad things already are or make you more confused. Or it can reveal that your crush likes you back. *No matter the outcome,* I believe you won't ruin anything worth keeping.

My years spent crushing on friends have taught me this well.

3 YOU NEVER DATED AND THEREFORE NEVER BROKE UP

My friendship with Ryan continued as we both wanted it to.

We went to a wooded area and sat down on two tree stumps that faced each other with five feet in between. As he prepared to recite his new poem for my feedback, he looked towards the sunset pouring like liquid through tangled branches. His soft face and strings of auburn hair were illuminated as he closed his eyes and thought.

I seized the opportunity to stare at him while he couldn't notice.

An old tree behind him cast shadows that contrasted with his pale, toned arms. Ryan mowed lawns as a side job, and I imagined his muscles tightening as he pushed mowers for hours at a time. He opened his eyes while turning his head away from the woods to look down at the worn path at his feet. His hair was lifted by the wind as it followed the turn of his head. His expression unreadable, I saw him the way I saw my dad: quiet and preoccupied.

After that evening, my mind replayed the clip, over and over, of Ryan's sun-kissed face turning back around. In the space of our silence, I imagined his heart telling mine that he loved me.

I later learned that the evening in the woods had been difficult for him—a girl he was getting to know had ended things right before we got together.

Ryan hadn't been thinking about me at all that evening—he'd been thinking about someone else.

My greatest idealizations have been on guy friends I was crushing on. It's difficult to describe this fantasy world, so just picture my crush coming down from the clouds dressed in white, thinking about me constantly and preparing himself for our eternal union.

Even his dating other girls is life experience and preparation for the relationship he'll eventually have with *me*… right?

Because you're not dating your friend, you can't break up. This leaves you with a disadvantage: it could take *forever* to become disillusioned with your friend and get over your feelings. While stuck in a friend-crush mire, you don't have much to do other than live in a fantasy world like the one I just described. If you have a vivid imagination like I do, you can take up residence there for a very long time.

The real problem lies in that there's not much that can destroy this fantasy world. Your friend-who-you're-not-dating often isn't doing the following (because you're not dating):

- Showing their true colors
- Picking fights with you
- Criticizing you

- Trying to change you
- Cheating on you
- Taking too long to commit
- Telling you they're not in love with you
- Breaking up with you

Because, you see, you're not dating your friend.

Kristin's Story

Jack called me up just before New Year's and asked me to the movies. He'd only been divorced for a year, and I knew his ex-wife. So, the idea of sitting in a dark theater with him was strange. I said no to the movie, so he invited me over for dinner and drinks instead. While at his house, he told me he was hoping to make some female friends. He asked me good questions, and we hit it off.

We began texting each other frequently, sharing YouTube links to music videos and exchanging a lot of witty banter. He got in touch with me more days than not and invited me over for Long Island iced teas and conversations about what he'd learned from his divorce and what I'd learned from being single.

His combination of openness and eye contact was electrifying. He made me feel like I was his favorite person in the world. I accepted his invitation to watch a movie with him at his house. We sat close to each other, but we didn't touch.

After months of ceaseless texting and some one-on-one time, I asked him what he thought was going on between us. I needed to know, especially because I'd seen him spending time with the girl down the street.

Across his small dining room table, with our Long Island Iced teas in hand, he said he saw me as someone he wanted to date "in the future" after he got to know me "a lot better." He added, "Who else do you know who has a connection like *we* do?"

"But," he continued, "I don't want anything *exclusive.*" He said there weren't any other women at that moment but me, but there could be "later on."

After hearing him out, I told him I felt I could do better than what he was offering.

"*Are* you doing better?" he countered.

I wish I had flipped him off right then... but I was falling for him.

He said, "Come on, give me a *chance.*"

I asked him if he was sure something wasn't going on with the girl down the street. He said they'd already explored the idea and decided against it.

"Okay," I said. "Since there aren't any other women right now, I will keep getting to know you better."

Jack and I continued texting frequently and occasionally eating and drinking at his dining room table. But nothing ever happened between us.

One day, while still getting to know Jack, I was at a neighborhood campfire attended by "the girl down the street." I noticed when looking over her shoulder that she and Jack were texting... a lot. I confronted Jack the next evening, but he denied that anything was going on with her.

I found out many months later that he was having one night stands with her while still spending time with me and texting me every day.

My friendship with Jack lasted a total of a year and a half until I concluded for sure that his actions didn't line up with his words. I later learned from some friends that Jack's version of the story is that he was "very clear" with me that he just wanted to be friends.

Ryan once dated a girl I know. She got to do all the things I'd wished I could do, like see him every night, watch movies with him, go hiking with him a heck of a lot more than I ever did, make out with him, and likely some other things that *I don't want to picture.*

After the relationship didn't work out, she told me that his emotional unavailability had been a big turn off and a deal breaker for her.

The friend you're crushing on might have some issues that would make dating a challenge. Or there could be less-than-healthy dynamics in your friendship. Have you noticed them?

Probably.

But even if you think your friend is a great catch, the fact is, if your friend doesn't want to date you then your friend is a terrible catch for you.

Think of it this way: if you and your friend can't even *begin* a dating relationship, why picture being in one at all? Your friend doesn't meet the most basic prerequisite for being more than friends, which is *wanting to be more than friends*.

Imagine the emptiness, loneliness, anxiety, frustration, lack of affection, and just plain misery if you were "dating" your friend who doesn't want to date you, after having forcefully dragged him or her into the relationship kicking and screaming.

Sounds like someone you'd need to break up with...

Danny finally figured this out.

> For years I was so in love with Kerry and believed we were perfect for each other—the only thing missing was her feelings. Everything else lined up; we had mutual friends, a shared passion for becoming successful artists, and an uncanny connection. It was like we were soul mates, and that was the biggest reason for my being in love with her. Some of our times together even felt like dates when we would

drink wine, talk, and laugh a lot after a long day of painting. She seemed to be having a better time with me than I imagined her having with anyone.

I envisioned our future romantic relationship going incredibly well and was waiting for her to realize she'd been in love with me all along. If only her feelings would get there, it seemed our bond would get us through anything.

A few years into our friendship, I had had a much-needed lightbulb moment and started questioning this fairy tale.

The lightbulb moment was this: if a romantic relationship with her could not even begin, how could it possibly ever be "great"?

Maybe it wouldn't be great at all. Maybe our friendship was going well precisely *because* we were only friends.

Danny, I also had such hopes for a fairy tale ending, and here's an *un*inspirational quote that sums up our pain:

> *If a dating relationship can't begin,*
>
> *then you can't be in it.*

Ouch.

Wait, the quote continues.

> *Even if you could be in it,*
>
> *it would suck.*

It is very difficult to stop idealizing the romantic relationship that you "will" be in with your friend. It seems as if your relationship will be utterly amazing once it begins.

But the strange truth is that a dating relationship that can't begin isn't real at all. And if it can't begin, then it can't exactly "go" great.

I wanted to kick myself when I finally realized that I'd been idealizing a romantic relationship with Ryan for *years*, a relationship that could never begin and may only last 48 hours even if it could.

My friendship with Ryan eventually settled into a pattern. We would get together a lot in the same week then perhaps not for a month. Or we'd get together every week for a while then I wouldn't hear from him for 6 weeks. Sometimes I feared I would never hear from him again. But I always did.

My being knee-deep in the friend zone with Ryan was an indication of what it might be like for me to date him. If dating him would be anything like being friends with him, then he'd sometimes be out of touch with me for weeks or even months. Given his lack of romantic feelings for me, he'd be disinterested, distant, and uncommitted—things that make relationships miserable. And who knows what other awful things the relationship could be? All I really know is, there can't be one. I must trust that the romantic distance between us is there for a reason.

It's hard to get over a crush on a friend when you never dated and therefore never broke up. So, here's just one step you can take to help you "break up" in your mind. Imagine dating your friend as your friend actually is—someone uninterested in dating you. Then write a "breakup" letter that you don't plan to give, stating to your friend that their disinterest is a deal breaker for you. Let them know also that there are other issues or dynamics between you two that are sabotaging the relationship, after using your observations to determine what these could be. Then conclude your letter by stating that this relationship, sadly, isn't going to work.

Case closed.

Then bury the letter in a park. For sentimentality's sake, bury it underneath the same bench where he told you he just wanted to be friends.

There *is* hope for you to get over your crush on your friend. I promise, because I succeeded in doing it. The biggest steps to doing so are in the next two chapters.

4 YOU DON'T KNOW WHETHER TO KEEP BEING FRIENDS

There wasn't much certainty along my journey of crushing on friends—at least not until the crushes had to end. It was a journey deep into myself and into my friendships, and I didn't know what I was going to find.

I don't know exactly what you'll find either. Your friend could shatter your heart into pieces when they meet their life partner (who isn't you). Your friend could introduce you to the real love of your life or to a new best friend. You could realize your friend is taking advantage of your feelings and get angry enough to finally let the friendship go. Your friend could be so kind to you that your brain gets permanently rewired. Or a combination of these things could happen.

You don't know until you know.

I used to want clear answers for everything and believed I could find them. I don't know when life started disappointing you in this realm, but for me, my late thirties, which just ended, was my phase of disillusionment. I used to think something was either clear or it was not; that something was either healthy or it was not. One of the things that showed me that this isn't always the case was my loooong-standing crush on Ryan.

Our friendship caused me confusion for years as I tried hard to figure out if he would ever fall in love with me. His ongoing interest in being my friend made me want to scale the heights of possibility. Had something changed? *Could* it change? Should I kiss him and see if his pheromones kick in and make him suddenly addicted to me? I feared, year after year, that these mental wheels would spin at the same speed for all eternity, stopped only by death.

When in the throes of this agony, I got advice from a couple of people. "Just don't hang out with him anymore."

Their advice was probably on target. But I didn't listen because I didn't yet understand the truth about my friendship with Ryan. I didn't know if our friendship was unhealthy or just *hard*. So in my ongoing uncertainty, I kept on being his friend.

I'm unable to regret the friendship when I look back over at how I've grown from it and the good things that happened as a result. Ryan never rejected me as a friend, even while I kept irrationally fearing he would, and this rewired my brain; I have less fear and less catastrophic thinking. We have introduced each other to new friends and new opportunities. We have helped shape and influence each other in positive ways. I believe he will always be in my life in some way, even if it's a small one going forward.

Yet I now know the deeper truth about our friendship. I'll tell you what that is in Chapter 5.

Katherine's Story

Eric is eight years younger than me, short and chubby with shoulder length stringy blonde hair. He is a gamer and wears a trench coat. Eric came across as someone who needed help—with his resume, his ego (it needed a boost), and his girl problems, which amounted to unrequited crushes on girls he met online who lived on other continents.

When Eric and I first met, he stared at me a lot, gravitated toward me at gatherings, and laughed *hard* at my jokes. He constantly commented on my witty Facebook posts, saying things like, "I can't stop laughing out loud." Soon, we were hanging out weekly with friends at his house and mine, listening to music, smoking Hookahs, and having intellectual conversations on our couches. He was a walking encyclopedia of historical and religious knowledge. He blinked at odd times. I found everything about him adorable in the light of his undying love and devotion to me (which he ultimately denied via email).

When I admitted to friends my crush on Eric, they looked at me like I had eight eyes. They thought Eric was immature, socially awkward, and refused to get a job. Those things were true, so I figured Eric should see *me* as a real catch.

My crush on Eric lasted too long. When it hit the 18-month mark, I knew something had to give, and soon. I had initially assumed his staring at me and heartily laughing at my jokes meant he liked me. But as time went on, he began opening up more and more about his crushes on girls overseas who refused to meet him. When I asked him in an email whether our friendship was getting too close, he replied that he enjoyed my company and didn't have any feelings for me beyond that.

My tormenting confusion over "what to do about Eric" finally resolved when he moved away and eventually stopped texting me.

It's hard to get over a crush on a friend when you don't know whether to keep being friends. Sometimes these situations resolve because your friend moves away, your friend gets married, or the friendship grows apart for another reason.

But when these resolutions don't come and the friendship stretches on and on, you must figure out the truth about your friendship.

Is my friendship with the guy I'm crushing on the height of maturity (*look how good I am at being friends with someone I'm in love with!*) or me reverting back to my childhood wish to overcome a detached parent? (It's the latter...) Do I secretly harbor an irrational gratitude? *Thank you* so much *for allowing me to be in love with you under the guise of friendship. You're the best*!

But it's not ever that my friend is "the best." It's that I'm in love with my friend and enamored with his every move and desperately imagining he feels the same way.

To muddy the waters further, friendship is the perfect disguise for a crush. My friend won't fault me for being "such a good friend." And I can convince myself that my motives are 100% pure, even heroic, as if I'll clean up after his wedding reception as the happy couple heads to the hotel room for night one of their honeymoon.

These muddy waters with each of my crushes have made me wonder if we should keep being friends.

Oh, *I* know! If I stop texting him, then maybe he'll stop texting me, and we can both put this charade behind us.

So, I remove him from my contacts and delete our text message thread. That way, I won't think of lame excuses to keep texting this guy whose wedding reception I could be cleaning up.

Except that strategy has backfired badly. With a couple of my friends, I removed and re-added their phone numbers so many times that I accidentally memorized them. Which meant I could easily text them even when their names weren't saved on my phone...

Back to impulsive texting.

Once, I assigned a friend his own special ringtone called *Danger Zone*—an ominous and face-paced tune to the sound of an obnoxiously loud alarm clock—and I hoped it would help me associate this guy with danger so that I'd stop texting him.

Unfortunately, this ring tone only served to trigger panic attacks and PTSD after I found out my friend had a secret girlfriend WHILE spending plenty of one-on-one time with me. *Fun times*.

But the friend you're crushing on may not be Mr. Danger Zone. Maybe your friend is a nice person. But no matter how *nice* your friend is, your mental health is on the fritz. Because being in love with your friend drives you crazy, but the prospect of *not* being friends makes you hopelessly sad.

This is a nice lead into my *un*inspirational quote for this chapter:

Some forks in the road present

two equally painful paths.

This quote is depressing, but I'll try to help take the edge off in the rest of this chapter. In the foggy world of *I don't know whether to keep being friends,* I can point to some road signs that emerged for me during my long, uncertain journey. The signs emerged in the fog of my own heart, taking a long time to become visible. I believe they will point you in the right direction. Exactly how you'll follow them is up to you.

The first road sign became visible when I was going back and forth about whether to keep spending time with one of my crushes. I gave him a lot: my time and adoration, help editing his philosophy papers, his favorite home-cooked meals, and endlessly flowing Bourbon. And what did I get in return? A steady diet of false hope.

I felt like this was a good trade off.

If you're crushing on a friend, you know exactly what I mean. You'll take all the false hope you can get, as long as you're not entirely convinced it's false. The hope feels really, *really* good, like a drug, and you keep going back for more.

My mom knew all I was giving to this friend, and she believed he was using me.

I told her that it was actually my fault because *I* was luring *him* into spending time with me by inviting him over to eat my food and *let* me edit his papers.

Her opinion of him was not improved when I told her he finished all my Bourbon and asked for my help perfecting his Bumble profile.

She had already told me to cut him off, but she knew I wouldn't do it. So, she said something different this time:

Keep hanging out until you're not enjoying it anymore

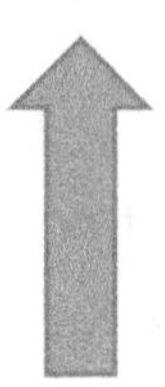

It was the only road sign I felt I could follow at that time, and my mom in her wisdom knew that. Taking my crushes' numbers out of my phone hadn't worked because it's really hard to cut a relationship out of our lives if we're enjoying it.

You can follow this road sign for a long, long time.

As long as your friend is still single.

As long as your friend lets you.

As long as both you and your friend are feeding on and enjoying your false hope.

Sadness hits me now that I know every moment of my hope about Ryan was false. The time I enjoyed with him was borrowed time. But I chose, again and again *for five years*, to sink into the present moments with him as if they'd lie still forever. I kept on following that road sign: *Keep hanging out until you're not enjoying it anymore.*

But you may not be able to follow it forever.

You could someday stop enjoying the friendship because of your deep fear of the truth. Or because your friend meets someone and leaves your romantic longings in the dust... and leaves you humiliated. You'll then come to a crossroads and need a different road sign to follow. Danny arrived there when he hit the seven-year mark in his friendship with Kerry.

There was always an opportunity to see Kerry; always a reason for us to text.

Whenever my paintings or hers got picked up by a gallery, we'd go see each other's work on display. Then there are the gallery receptions and the parties afterwards. Of course, I'd help her set up her art shows, and if I wanted help with mine, she'd oblige. Even if I didn't have a reason to text her on a given day, it wasn't hard to come up with one—perhaps she had something I wanted to borrow. Then there were our gatherings with mutual friends, many of whom are also artists.

Our friendship drove me crazy, but it was incredibly "worth" it to me. I was terrified of losing Kerry's friendship. In my mind, the only thing worse than not marrying her was not having her in my life at all. I lived in fear that she would see that I was still hung up on her. I was also on pins and needles that she'd start dating someone; even worse, that she'd get married. Yet I would need to be happy for her if she did.

Kerry didn't text me often, but then she would, when I least expected it, and I'd breathe a big sigh of relief. I'd get my courage back up to invite her to my place, and she was almost always free to come over for another evening of art, conversation, and wine. We'd have such an amazing time that I would be on a high for days afterwards.

Then I'd crash hard because I had to face reality all over again—Kerry was just a friend and might never become my wife. The fear would start back up that I might not hear from her again. But then we'd reconnect. And the cycle of euphoria, crashing, and fear would start all over.

When she dated one of our mutual friends for six months, I thought it might kill me.

It took me years to question whether this emotional and mental cycle was really worth it. I started imagining what it might be like to let Kerry go; to stop contacting her, to stop approaching her as much at gatherings. To cease caring who she met and dated. It felt freeing to start thinking that way.

It was like something slowly eased in for the first time since I'd met Kerry...something lots of other people have already. It's called *self-esteem*.

That brings us to our second road sign.

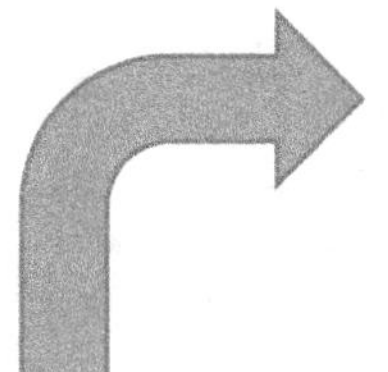

Self-esteem

As in, you will need to get more of it if you want to come upon clear skies.

Let's address the "not enjoying it anymore" part of "Keep hanging out until you're not enjoying it anymore." If you are enjoying your connection with your crush even while going insane, then first of all, I understand *so well*. Secondly, I've noticed that people with self-esteem don't keep doing that forever.

Here's just a tiny sample of the unending maze my mind used to wander through with Ryan:

Could he ever like me? Maybe he's falling for me right now, right when he wasn't expecting to. Or maybe he hates me and that's why he didn't respond to that text. Should I invite him over this Friday night? No, that's too soon; I should wait at least two more weeks before inviting him over again. Does he think I still like him, or does he think I'm over him? Does he think I came to the party because I knew he'd be there?

What did it mean that he didn't pull his arm away when I accidentally brushed against it?

Then I would replay an imaginary conversation that had unfortunately been on "repeat" in my head far too many times—the one where Ryan says, "Can we talk?" and he tells me he is starting to have feelings for me, and I tell him that I still like him *a lot* but don't think we should date because I'm afraid he won't be able to see it through and I don't want to ruin the friendship trying or get my heart broken beyond repair. Of course, I'm a lot wordier than that in these imaginary conversations, because being wordier means getting to spend *more* time with him...

But it's a worthless imaginary conversation because he DOESN'T like me in that way and is never going to say, "Can we talk?" about *anything at all* and... are you bored yet, hearing me ramble? I am too.

Because the thing about these run-on circular thoughts is that they are a huge distraction from my actual life. And people with self-esteem don't enjoy these one-sided fictions taking too much of their headspace.

When the universe teaches us lessons, it doesn't care how long it takes. Your first grey hairs can appear. Your crush on your friend could hit the five-year then 10-year then 30-year mark. When all of your hair is grey and you're still crushing on your friend, you'll wonder why the universe didn't stop you. The truth is that it whispered again and again, gently nudging you to respect yourself. You didn't listen, yet it still just whispered. You're allowed to waste your life in false hope; no one has the power to stop this but you. If you persist in enjoying an unrequited crush on a friend and never take the direction of self-esteem, the pain will someday scream loud like a megaphone. You'll wish you'd listened back when the warnings were whispers.

Self-esteem is hard to pin down. We can think about it and talk about it yet still not actually get it. I can best describe it as a still, small voice that came to me, just once in a while, and suggested that the crush I was entertaining was not worth my time and my heart; that I didn't need it in my life after all; that I could close the door on it at any moment and move on. This voice gently and oh-so-quietly told me that I am better than that, that I should stop placing such a cheap price tag on my heart.

I heard that small voice so many times that I started considering what it said.

This led to finally believing it. Then I started changing my behavior. Changing my behavior reinforced the truth of that voice, making it louder.

When I say "changing my behavior," I mean that there came points with each of my crushes on friends—yes, even with Ryan—when I stopped contacting them. I really did. *I stopped contacting them.* And *then* I finally knew without any doubt that I was too good to entertain those unrequited crushes.

I won't tell you to stop contacting your crush, because I get that you have to arrive at that decision on your own.

But I *will* say, loud and clear, this next road sign:

Hang out in moderation.

I'm about to give you my most prized insight. After years of education, personal study, keen observations, numerous crushes, fervent prayers for deliverance, crying until my ribs hurt, and even believing I was "cursed," I emerged with a ground-breaking piece of wisdom. It wasn't easy to come by. All the awareness in the world didn't produce it. It was a realization that came only as I changed my *behavior*. It has been my golden ticket, and I'm so glad we have reached the point of my sharing it with you.

Are you ready? Hold on tight...

The less contact you have with your friend, the more easily you'll get over your crush.

Imagine that.

Hang out with your friend, *at most*, in moderation.

Do not spend too much time with your friend; that's crazy making. Even if you were somewhat sane once, you won't be any more if this is what you're doing. This road sign is the clearest one of all. Don't crash into it then blame the fog. Don't be like someone I know who was so attached to her friend that she gave him morning wake up calls... Every. Single. Morning. He welcomed them. When he met someone and got married, she was blindsided and devastated and her mental health took a very downward turn. But we won't go there, because this book is meant to be *un*inspiring, not traumatizing.

You can make the path of friendship with your crush less painful by scaling the friendship back, often *way* back. Give yourself enough time between contact to recover from the flood of false-hope-turned-ecstasy and subsequent emotional crashing. I endured this cycle of ecstasy and crashing enough times to realize I don't want it in my life. Another time I needed to scale back was when one of my crushes got a girlfriend and I was consumed with jealousy whenever he mentioned her. Being that jealous meant I was too attached and too invested in my friend. Solution? I stopped trying to see him as often. By scaling back, I have been able to remain friends, *casually*, with some of my crushes.

Sometimes the only way out of the craziness is out of the friendship entirely. Yes, zero contact is an option. I used to think that ending a friendship with a crush was unthinkable. I was proud—for years—to be the "cool" girl who could "handle" having an intense crush on a friend and being "fine" with "whatever" the future would hold while I "enjoyed" the friendship and "lived in the moment" and... the number of words in quotes that expose my folly drives my point deep into the ground.

I finally let go of Mr. Danger Zone, but I held onto my friend-on-Bumble albeit while scaling the friendship way back. Although I enjoy his company when we run into each other, I no longer contact him. My false hope that he'd fall in love with me faded like cheap clothing in a washing machine every time my heart went through the cycle of hope and disappointment. And this points us to the final road sign:

Give Up Hope

What I really mean is, give up *false* hope.

I started this chapter saying there wasn't much certainty along my journey of crushing on friends—at least not until the end. I have certainty now, and I would have had it sooner if I'd been willing to see what the signs and patterns were telling me.

Speaking of signs and patterns...

Look deeply at signs and patterns that your friend doesn't like you in that way—that your friend isn't the person your fantasy is projecting. And then give up hope. That is, give up false hope. To help you do that, we're going to tackle false hope and fantasy head on in the last chapter of this book.

Hope is a beautiful thing. You want to hold onto it. And you can best do that by giving up false hope—its counterfeit. When you recognize then let go of false hope, which isn't serving you, true hope for something real can takes its place.

5 YOU'RE LIVING IN A FANTASY

Don't fall for Ryan Miller. Don't fall for Ryan Miller, I said to myself like a mantra the day I fell in love with him. I had noticed him and chatted with him around campus in the two years before that day and hadn't been able to stop thinking about him. So I was primed to fall for him the moment I got a chance.

Which, as you know now, was when he stopped me and explained his poetry project on the campus lawn, sparking our long-held friendship. His dark jeans hung loosely over his toned torso as he leaned back against a tree with his hands in his pockets. He'd said he knew I was a writer and wanted my help.

After we parted on the lawn, he emailed me an audio file of poems he had recorded. It was a spring day, and I was going to listen to them one by one.

So I rested in my backyard hammock staring at the ascending branches and leaves above me, pondering the silent, still life that was behind the vibrant movements of nature. My ear buds hooked up to my phone, I pulled up the file, touched the first one, and pressed "play."

It was a beautiful day to fall in love. Shaded under the tree, I watched the sun glisten around the outlines of green and yellow swaying leaves. I relaxed in order to feel weightless as I fell.

Because whenever I told myself not to fall for someone, I didn't listen.

One of his poems was about falling in love in the spring... ironically. I listened to it on repeat, mesmerized by his vulnerability and clever rhyming. I wondered the trails of his voice as I pictured him reciting the words.

I didn't know where Ryan's voice ended and he began. I didn't know where he ended and I began. From my hammock, the world was one; the sun and leaves above me, his words within me, him within his words, and me within him.

I didn't yet care whether my love for him was a fantasy. I was grateful to be in love.

I've brought up fantasy several times already because it's the cornerstone of an unreturned crush on a friend.

Fantasy is involved in each of my chapters. You fantasize that your friendship is the perfect foundation for the romance you "will" someday have. You fantasize that keeping silent about your feelings is helping your friend fall in love with you... or that your friend will come around if you professed your feelings already. Although a romantic relationship never seems to begin, you fantasize it will someday "be" amazing. You don't know whether to keep being friends because your friendship is so intertwined with your fantasy. And here we are in chapter 5, and it's time to burst your bubble like it's never been burst before.

I've always taken pride in being someone who faces the truth head on.

Except when I've been knee deep in a crush on a friend. In those cases, I was like any addict: I just wanted to feel good. Fantasy seemed like a secure holding place for my longings. It kept them "safe" until the day that the glorious future would finally unveil itself.

Don't think fantasy isn't a drug. It will wrap itself around every neuron in your brain and make you feel like you can get through anything. It blankets the ground of your soul so that you always have a warm place to lie. While soaking up the warmth of your fantasy, you can tell yourself anything you want: "We're always going to be just friends" and "I just want him to be happy" and "I know he doesn't like me back and that's okay." You can even believe yourself. But the *real* reason you feel fine is because you're still wrapped up in your fantasy; the future hasn't happened yet, so your false hope is flowing like a river through your bloodstream.

Fantasy is an invisible addiction. But it's there, and you're taking a hit whenever you need one.

For years, I had regular "hits" to keep my fantasy going: Ryan and I talking on campus; texting each other links to poems and new trails we wanted to try; gatherings with mutual friends; hikes and one-on-one time at each other's houses. Even if we went a few weeks without contact, it only took one mundane text message from him, or his reply to one of mine, to give me a fresh "hit" and keep my fantasy going.

You can tell yourself you're fine and okay with "whatever the future holds," but you won't really feel fine and okay when you can't get more of the drug. For me, that point came when Ryan entered a serious relationship. He'd still come over when I asked him to, but spending time with him while knowing he had a girlfriend wrecked me. My fantasy and false hope began unraveling like they never had with him before.

A relationship coach helped me analyze my friendship with Ryan in the wake of his new girlfriend. A knife twists my insides as I put the truth into words: I practiced a pattern of relating to Ryan that was second nature to me when I was a child. It begins with a vast emptiness and longing and leads to fantasizing that a connection is much greater than it is. I now believe that Ryan and I bonded over a fantasy relationship. I fantasized he would someday love me in the way I most wanted to be loved. He fantasized that I was there for him to fall back on when he needed to feel better.

This realization left me sobbing in the cold, feeling exiled from the home I had made with him in my heart.

Janna's Story

Sam and I had mutual friends at our graduate school, and I noticed he came over to talk to me a lot after class. I later learned that was because he had a crush on my friend Jenny who was almost always by my side. At the time, though, I thought Sam might like *me* since he was always coming around.

Sam is short with a round face and a charming smile, which I got to see a lot because the thing Sam is best at is being hilarious. He may be the wittiest person I've ever met. I'd sometimes be laughing days later when I replayed his comments in my head.

Sam's parents are both Sociology professors who live in a very nice neighborhood, and I was fascinated imagining what Sam's childhood was like around their fancy dinner table with his younger sisters and his parents. What did they talk about? Their conversations must have been intelligent and interesting, and I wanted to be transported back in time and be their invisible guest. I was envious of his childhood that seemed so much more structured than mine had been.

Jenny and I joined a book club with Sam and some of our other friends, so I got to see him every week for our book discussion in addition to talking with him after class and at the university cafeteria.

I had a couple of fears. The first was that Sam is six years younger than me. I didn't know if he minded that. Second, I had come from a broken home and wondered if he only liked girls who came from families like his.

Nevertheless, I was so smitten with Sam that I could barely walk a straight line. I started picturing our wedding day. I imagined myself in photos with him and his family, taken at holidays like Easter and Christmas. I imagined his sisters and me becoming good friends. Lastly, I envisioned myself at the dinner table with his whole family, the mystery of their dinner conversations unveiled.

This fantasy went on for about eight months until the anticipation of my future was more than I could bear. I needed to know if this dream was coming true. I looked at a calendar in my bedroom and flipped to November and wrote down, "Ask him out for coffee." November was two months away.

My palms were sweating and my heart was racing as November got close. I was working up the nerve to call Sam, and I was banking on my life changing when I did.

On November 1st, I picked up the phone and dialed his number, and when he answered I said the words I had rehearsed so many times. He agreed to coffee with me the following Saturday morning.

The day before our date, I said after class, "Are you still on for coffee tomorrow morning?"

There was something about the way he looked at me that told me he'd hoped I'd forgotten.

But he said, "Sure. I'll see you then."

We did indeed have coffee the next morning.... *for three hours.*

I thought it was going really well until about two and a half hours in. At that point, Sam confessed he had a crush on my friend Jenny and asked me if I could help him get a date with her.

One of my favorite quotes is:

"Reality can be described as what we humans run into when we are wrong, a collision in which we always lose."[ii]

Reality will eventually crash into your fantasy. Do you want to see the truth now, or you do you want your fantasy to violently crumble against your will later on? You'll be in a lot more pain than you ever dared suspect back when you were wrapping your fantasy around you like a warm sweater.

Fantasy is tricky when it uses material from reality and warps it into something it's not. In our fantasies, we see real people with their real words and actions. But we can imagine a burning love and devotion behind it all that isn't there.

Obviously, my mind struggles to ward off fantasy when it comes to crushes on friends. Fantasy was a coping mechanism for me when, as a child, my dad ignored me almost all the time. My mom tried to do the right thing by telling my siblings and me, "Your dad loves you in the best way he knows how."

So, when my dad ignored me, I fantasized that he was wishing for a relationship but didn't know how to tell me. When I got tiny crumbs of attention from him, they felt like a feast.

Then in my crushes on friends I fantasized they were secretly pining for me. Then the attention I got from them, which was always much more than I ever got from my dad, looked a lot like imminent marriage proposals. The sad truth is, any fantasy that I "loved" my friend was really a fantasy that *he loved me.*

My *un*inspirational quote, folks, is this:

> *Fantasy thrives where*
>
> *reality disappoints.*

You don't need fantasy when reality is satisfying.

There can even be an inverse relationship between the wasteland of reality and the euphoria of fantasy. So, if you are in a cloud-nine fantasy about your friend, the inverse reality is likely pretty bleak.

I wanted my crush on Ryan to be my secret to enjoy without anyone's input. So, I didn't tell most of my friends. And at least three of them had crushes on Ryan, too—he's a real heartthrob. I understand how hard it is to talk to anyone who might discourage you from entertaining a crush on a friend.

I ultimately told my mom, my sister, and my relationship coach the story of my friendship with Ryan in exhausting detail— all the signs he didn't like me and all the signs that he might. I told them about professing my feelings in the past and him gently letting me down. All three of them concluded he was not in love with me, no matter how much time we'd spent together over the years. This same coach was the one who helped me see that Ryan and I connected over a fantasy relationship.

This could be your situation, too. Have you considered that your friend you're crushing on is *also* living in a fantasy... with *you*? But it's not the same fantasy. You're fantasizing that your friend will fall in love with you, while your friend is fantasizing that you'll always be there to fall back on as a crutch, a security blanket, or perhaps even a plan B. If indeed you two are connecting over a fantasy relationship, then the fantasy serves you both in different ways. You feed each other's fantasy so that you can each continue it for your own psychological security. But in the long run, you will disappoint each other.

What other possible truths is your fantasy protecting you from? Is your friend using you? Are you two holding each other back? Perhaps your friend would break your heart if you dated. Perhaps deep down you know that *you* would end things if you dated. Your relationship could end in divorce if you married. Maybe you don't even want to date your friend; your romantic fantasy is just there to shield you from dissatisfaction with your life or fears about your future.

Whatever the case may be, awareness alone won't fix it. You have to get tired of the fantasy. It has to finally cause you more pain than pleasure as you feel threatened by the terrifying reality that your fantasy is crumbling. If this eats at you long enough, you'll realize it is time to take serious action, to do some damage control.

Danny ultimately felt tormented by the thought that his fantasy was not going to come true. He had to decide whether to let it go.

Seven years into my crush on Kerry, I wrestled with whether to keep believing my "vision" of she and I getting married-the one I'd had minutes after I met her.

I wanted to hold onto hope so that our "love story" would become more and more epic. I imagined being married to Kerry and telling people, "It was *year seven*, right when I was about to give up hope..." It was a beautiful love story, in my head—one that would end well against all odds. At that point, I'd finally be able to tell Kerry, and others, about my "vision."

Yet I was tired of the same mental confusion. I started feeling like I was setting myself up for major depression.

It was mind boggling because, theoretically, there *was* still hope. There would, in fact, never be a time when there wasn't hope. Even if Kerry gets married someday, she could become divorced or widowed and then fall in love with me. So, you see, there is always hope if you're looking at this theoretically.

But theory is often not reality.

I finally realized that there is only one way to give up hope, and it's to *decide*---make a free decision and take responsibility for it. The existentialists would have loved me.

It's hard to get over a crush on a friend when you're living in a fantasy. Sometimes the only thing we can do to let go of a fantasy is *decide*.

So, what happened to Danny and Kerry? He let go of the fantasy of marrying Kerry after his crush reached the seven-year mark. For him, this meant letting go of his cycle of initiating contact with her except for once in a great while if there was truly a good reason. He cried for weeks after letting it go.

It is year 11 since they met. Kerry is in a relationship. She and Danny are still casual friends, but they have much less contact than they used to. Danny is still attracted to Kerry yet would say that he no longer has an active crush on her.

Danny tells me he learned so much from his crush on Kerry that he wouldn't crush on a friend like that again. It's not worth it, he said.

Fantasy is an unsafe playground. In the end, it will cut you. You should get out sooner rather than later. Fantasy doesn't deliver what it promises—that's what makes it a fantasy.

If I'd read a chapter like this years ago, I likely would not have heeded it. I would have been sitting at this same desk where I sit now, counting the hours until Ryan and I got into his jeep and headed to a state park on a Friday afternoon after class. I would have been texting him to see if he could bring an extra water bottle for me.

But Ryan wasn't the love of my life, as I'd imagined he was all those years.

And fantasy wasn't my friend.

AFTERWARD

I let go of my crush on Ryan in the same way that Danny let go of his crush on Kerry. It was very turbulent watching my long-held fantasy disintegrate in front of my eyes, leaving me with what I had hoped to escape from—the truth.

The worst part was the anticipation of my fantasy dying. But after I let it die, I was free from my fantasy. Free doesn't always mean happy, though, especially at first. All I could see for a while was a nailed coffin containing my unrequited crush, the dead hope never to be resurrected. Unfortunately, I also suffered from intense anxiety and feelings of dread anytime I saw him with his girlfriend or feared situations where I might run into them. I knew my suffering would last for a while, and I lamented that I had brought it on myself.

Yet even in the midst of my grief, I understood that I hadn't really lost anything. My friendships are still there in some form, along with their beautiful memories. With them are my painful and hard-earned lessons. I hold them close by my side. They'll never leave me, and they are taking me into a better future. So I cannot regret my crushes on friends. They have helped me to grow and to see both them and me as we really are.

I wanted to know just how close I could get to these friends I had feelings for. How far inside their souls and lives would they let me go, and what would I find there? Back when I was trying to win Ryan over, a friend used to tell me that I needed to do the "arm touch"—put my hand on his arm and let it linger. I wouldn't do it because I was afraid his arm would flinch and that he would move it away. But recently, I finally put my hand on Ryan's arm for a couple of seconds at a party. It was my way of inching a little bit closer to someone whose friendship taught me so much, now that I've made peace that we won't ever be more than friends.

It's what we are all doing. Finding our deepest pain that we have projected onto the faces and arms of those around us and seeing how we might overcome it—how we might inch closer to it and make it smaller. Make it end happier. Make it something other than it was long ago.

Along those lines, my dad's aftershave has lost its mystique, and I don't see his face in the faces of my friends so much anymore. I've learned that my friends are human just like me. Their scented steam has shrunk from the size of the earth down to the size of a small bathroom.

My pain, too, will continue to shrink, as I move through my grief of letting go of a five-year crush. I'm not a gaping hole of pain, as I used to feel I was when these things happened, but rather a beautiful soul who has learned the hard way that I'm too valuable to stay stuck in a crush on a friend.

You picked up this book because you have reasons to believe you need to get over a crush on a friend. So, I've assumed in this book that your crush is unrequited. I would love to be wrong, but here we are.

I hope each chapter of my book has helped you see your situation more clearly and make progress on your journey. I wish you more and longer strides than I made as you move on from your crush on your friend. I am happy about what may be waiting for you on the other side of your crush. If nothing else, you will find that you are in a stronger and more loving relationship with yourself and hold yourself in higher esteem than you did before.

Dignity and self-esteem always come into play when we're stuck in crushes on friends. We come to forks in the road where we can either grovel at their feet or we can stop mystifying them.

When you come to these forks in the road, decide that you are more important. Decide that every moment of your newfound self-esteem is more miraculous than this friendship ever was. Make decisions that prove you deserve better than a fantasy; better than a friendship in which you're not on the same page.

Don't feast on false hope. You can do better. When you behave as if you know that, you send a very powerful message to yourself and everyone around you—a message that declares your dignity and worth.

It's a message no one can refute.

QUICK HELP

I have shared stories, quotes, and insights with you throughout my book. But I totally get that you want some concrete help. So in the following pages you'll find just that: a checklist of signs that your crush on your friend is something you would benefit from leaving behind, a summary of this book's advice, my two favorite book recommendations related to this topic, and relationship coaches I recommend.

Let-Go Checklist

Do you worry that your crush on your friend might be unhealthy? Is it time to consider letting it go? Check all of the below signs that are true for you. The more signs you check, the more likely it is that you will benefit from the advice in this book.

- ☐ I often fantasize about a romantic future with my friend.
- ☐ I often create reasons to contact and see my friend.
- ☐ My crush on my friend preoccupies my mind.
- ☐ I'm too in love with my friend to consider other dating prospects.
- ☐ We are not just casual friends; we are "good friends."
- ☐ I'm enamored with the friendship connection we have.
- ☐ I feel like my friend "gets" me more than others do.

- ☐ My friend doesn't like me "in that way."
- ☐ My friend is not pursuing a romantic relationship with me.
- ☐ My friend benefits from the things I offer and give.
- ☐ My friend knows about my feelings and doesn't mind.
- ☐ My mind goes in the same circles trying to "figure out" my romantic future with my friend.
- ☐ My emotions cycle between hope and disappointment.
- ☐ My feelings for my friend have lasted over a year.
- ☐ My mental health is suffering because of my feelings for my friend.
- ☐ I feel possessive of my friend.
- ☐ I usually hide my crush from others so that they won't discourage me.
- ☐ I am jealous when my crush dates or shows romantic interest in other people.
- ☐ I feel like letting go of this friendship would be devastating.

☐ I believe my friend will come around and fall for me.

☐ My friend and I largely avoid the topic of my feelings.

☐ My friend doesn't reciprocate my feelings, but I won't give up.

☐ I live for the excitement of hearing from and seeing my friend again.

☐ My friend seems less invested in our friendship than I am.

☐ My friend is just as invested in our friendship as I am but for reasons that do not involve romantic interest.

☐ I will be heartbroken if my friend enters a serious relationship with someone else.

Advice

- Don't let inspirational quotes and other people's love stories lead you into false hope that you will marry your friend. You could marry a friend someday, but it may not be the one you are crushing on right now.

- What option gives you more peace: professing your feelings to your friend, or not professing your feelings? Listen to yourself and to what friends and family suggest. I don't believe you will lose anything worth keeping if you decide to share your feelings.

- If you have already shared your feelings with your friend and they are not reciprocated, believe your friend the first time. Don't wait or hope for your friend's mind to change. It's possible that your friend's mind *could* change, but you don't need to stay invested in your friendship for that to happen.

- A helpful concrete step to getting over your crush could be writing a "breakup" letter that you don't plan to give, stating to your friend that their disinterest is a deal breaker for you. Let them know what other issues are sabotaging the relationship, using your observations to imagine what those could be. Then conclude your letter by stating that this relationship isn't going to work.

- If you want to keep hanging out with your friend as long as you are enjoying it, do so. But if you're mental health has been suffering, listen to the still small voice that gently suggests you are too valuable to do this to yourself. Scale the friendship back so that you are only hanging out in moderation, at most.

- Let go of the false hope that your friend is going to come around and fall in love with you. Understand that true hope is too valuable to be replaced with false hope. When you give up false hope, you can regain hope for something to come into your life that can actually work out.

- Journal about the fantasy you have about your friend. What is the fantasy? What are all the things it involves? What is the fantasy doing for you? What is it numbing you from feeling? What harmful effects does this fantasy have on you now or could have on you in the future? Using these insights, try to see *through* your fantasy instead of with it.

Further Reading

Attached: The New Science of Adult Attachment and How It Can Help You Find—and Keep—Love by Amir Levine and Rachel Heller

Deeper Dating by Ken Page

The Soulmate Shortcut by Orna and Matthew Walters, available through their website https://www.creatingloveonpurpose.com/

Relationship Coaches

Jane Garapick

Getting to TRUE Love

https://gettingtotruelove.com/

Orna and Matthew Walters

Creating Love on Purpose

https://www.creatingloveonpurpose.com/

*Un*inspirational Quotes:

*"What screws us up the most in life
is the picture in our head of what
it's supposed to be."*[iii]

*Someone else's love story could be
your false reality.*

*Telling the truth can't make things bad but it
can show you how bad things already are.*

*If a dating relationship can't begin, then you
can't be in it. Even if you could be in it,
it would suck.*

*Some forks in the road present
two equally painful paths.*

*"Reality can be described as what we
humans run into when we are wrong, a
collision in which we always lose."*[iv]

Fantasy thrives where reality disappoints.

If you enjoyed this book, please take a minute to rate and review it on Amazon. As a self-published author, the only ones getting this book out there are me and possibly you. Ratings go a long way in helping this book get discovered.

Thank you!

-Cara

ABOUT THE AUTHOR

Cara Menae Miller has a master's degree in Clinical Counseling. Her favorite subjects are philosophy, religion, and psychology, which she studies for pleasure. She especially loves analyzing people and relationships. In her free time, she enjoys nature walks, rollerblading, cooking, reading, writing, and spending time with friends, family, and children. She's a highly sensitive person and is passionate about lifestyle choices that honor sensitivity. *How to Get Over a Crush on a Friend* is her third book. Her first book is called *How to End a Friendship Nicely: An Approach for Highly Sensitive People*. Her second book is a quote journal for highly sensitive people called *My HSP Journal*.